Little Tourist: A Cystic Fibrosis Adventure

Written by:
Alice Abou-Chakra

Illustrated by:
TullipStudio

01

To Natalie, Roger, Isabelle, and James, thank you for giving me a life full of love and being there for me through all the highs and lows of living with cystic fibrosis. Thank you for sharing so many happy memories and supporting my dream of creating this book.

I am truly grateful to all those who have worked tirelessly to help the cystic fibrosis community.

I wouldn't be here today without you.

NOT EVERYONE WITH CYSTIC FIBROSIS IS THE SAME, AND WHAT MAY BE RECOMMENDED FOR ONE PERSON MAY NOT BE SUITABLE FOR ANOTHER. PLEASE DISCUSS THIS WITH YOUR MEDICAL TEAM BEFORE CONSIDERING TAKING PART IN ANY EXTREME ACTIVITIES OR DECIDING TO GO ABROAD.

My name is Alice, I have cystic fibrosis. A sweat test when I was a baby gave me this diagnosis.

Let's shorten it to CF to make things easy. I need enzymes to digest food. My cough is crackled and wheezy.

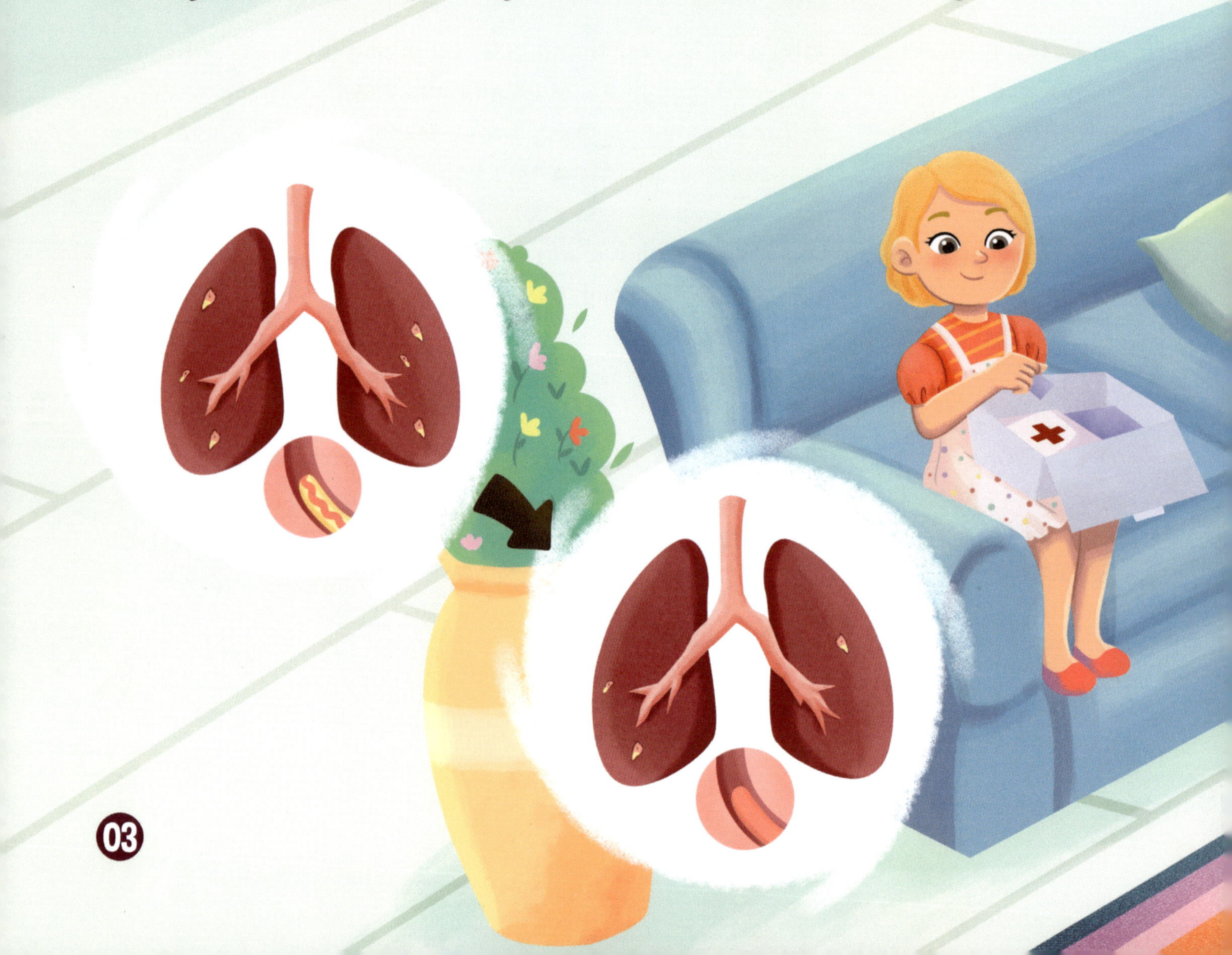

Between me and my sister Isabelle, only I have the special CF gene. This gives me sticky mucus, so I have daily treatments to keep my lungs clean.

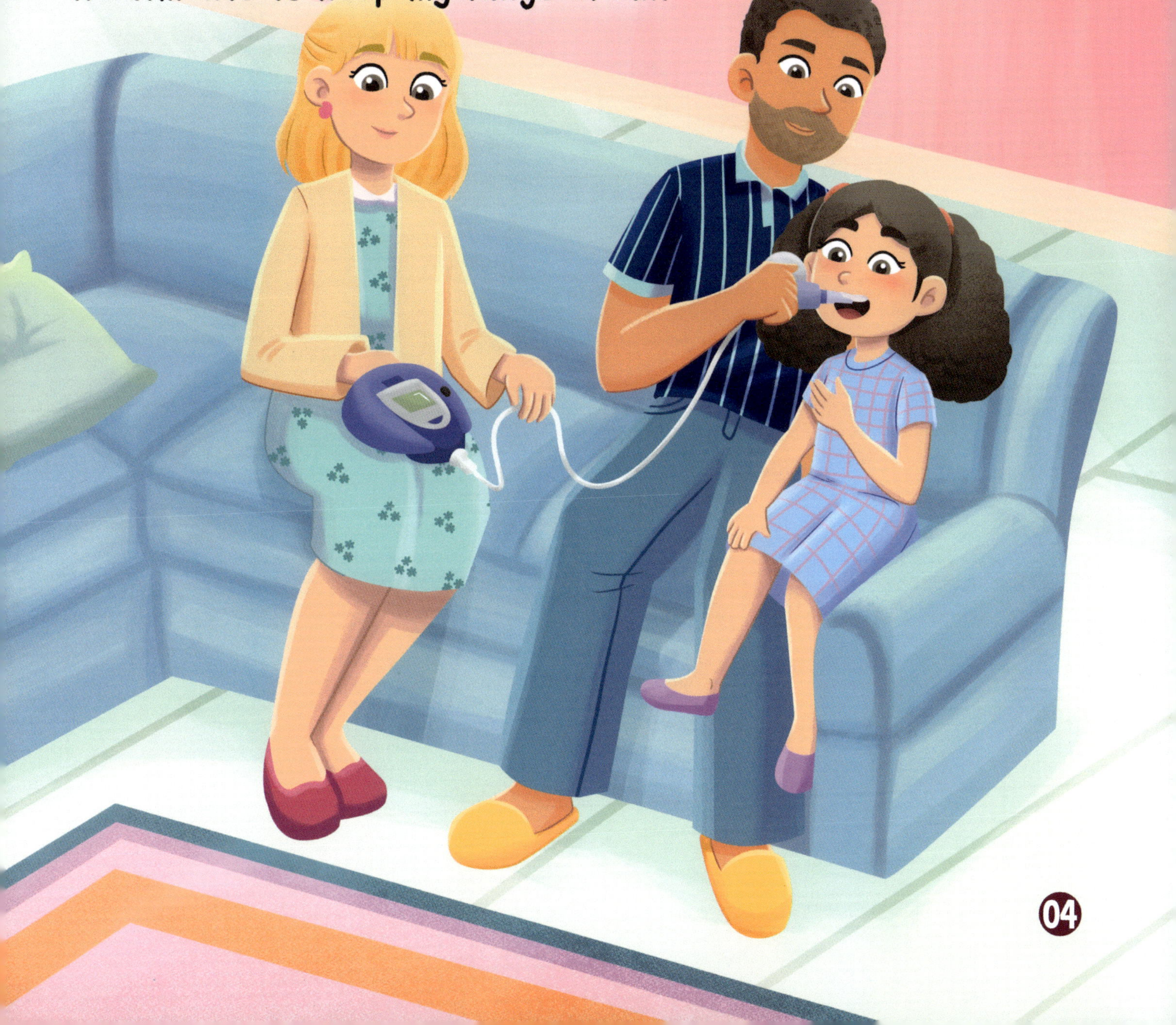

I've had a dream since I was a little girl...
...to fly on an aeroplane and see the whole wide world.

It's a bit more difficult because I have CF...
...but nothing's impossible. I've just got to follow a few steps.

First, let's talk to Dr. K, and see what he's got to say. "Hi Alice, it's good to see you. How are you feeling today?"

I am great! I have been doing my breathing treatments everyday. Hoping that if I'm well enough, I can go on holiday.

"If you never miss a treatment and get your lung function in its normal range... I'll give you a 'fit to fly' letter to go on holiday in exchange."

I've finished my physio, coughed the mucus out of my chest.

I blow into my lung function machine, and the result is at its best.

Dr. K, I've done all the steps and I'm feeling a lot better. Now please, can I get my signed 'fit to fly' letter?

We've got a round-the-world ticket for 6 countries, with lots of exploring to do.

We will visit France, Australia, Egypt, Kenya, The USA, and Iceland too!

We get through the airport after queuing up for a while.

The security guard looks at my 'fit to fly' letter with a smile.

He says, "You can go through, have a safe flight."

We show our passports at the gate. I'll be in France tonight!

In the cold snowy mountains, my fingers have frozen.
I wrap up in winter clothes, I love the ski boots
I've chosen.

I will meet an instructor, who will teach me how to ski. We swish and we swoosh down the ski slope with glee.

Australia has the world's largest coral reef. It's so big and beautiful that I'm in disbelief.

I've got a 'safe to scuba dive' form signed by Dr. K. Look, gliding gracefully underwater is a stingray!

In the Egyptian desert is a mountain.
I want to hike to the top!

I've tried hiking once before,
but I was unwell and had to stop.

I'm back to try again.
I start slow with a stroll.

A puff of my blue inhaler keeps
my breathing under control.

In the plains of Kenya, we drive in a safari jeep...
...where giraffes and zebras gallop, and big lions sleep.

I drink water, take salt tablets, wear a hat and suncream..

This is to stay hydrated as the heat can be extreme.

I'm having so much fun on my round-the-world-trip!
But today it's harder to breathe. I'm starting to feel sick.

Iceland is a country that's known as the land of fire and ice. Volcanoes erupt lava...Don't go too close is my only advice. If you look up at the dark night sky, pretty lights are revealed.

Our sun's energy dances with our planet's magnetic field.
There are green and pink colours, so beautiful and bright.
The name of this natural wonder is the northern lights.

Having cystic fibrosis can be hard sometimes, and it's okay to be sad. But it makes me a strong warrior, so it's not all that bad.

Look at all the amazing things around the world I've seen! It doesn't matter that I had to have hospital treatment in-between.

You can follow your dreams too, if you look after yourself. Because the top priority that comes first must always be your health.

Travel Wish List

The True Story

Alice was diagnosed with cystic fibrosis at the age of 7, and like many CF patients of the 1990's, her parents were told Alice probably wouldn't see her 18th birthday.

Medical advancements have greatly improved her quality of life, and at the time of writing this book Alice is 30 years old. For as long as Alice can remember, she wanted to leave her hometown in Wales, UK, to explore the world.

It involved a lot of organisation for Alice and her medical team to arrange an extra stock of medication and get her medical equipment ready to take away with her. For Alice, it was worth the difficulties because it meant she could fulfil her dream of travelling the world.

She embarked on her first backpacking trip at 22 years old through Southeast Asia, and her passion for travel only grew from there. Alice continued her travels throughout the world, with frequent visits back home for hospital check-ups and IV treatment at least once a year.

Her goal is now to advocate for children with cystic fibrosis to never give up hope and always follow their dreams, no matter how difficult they may seem.

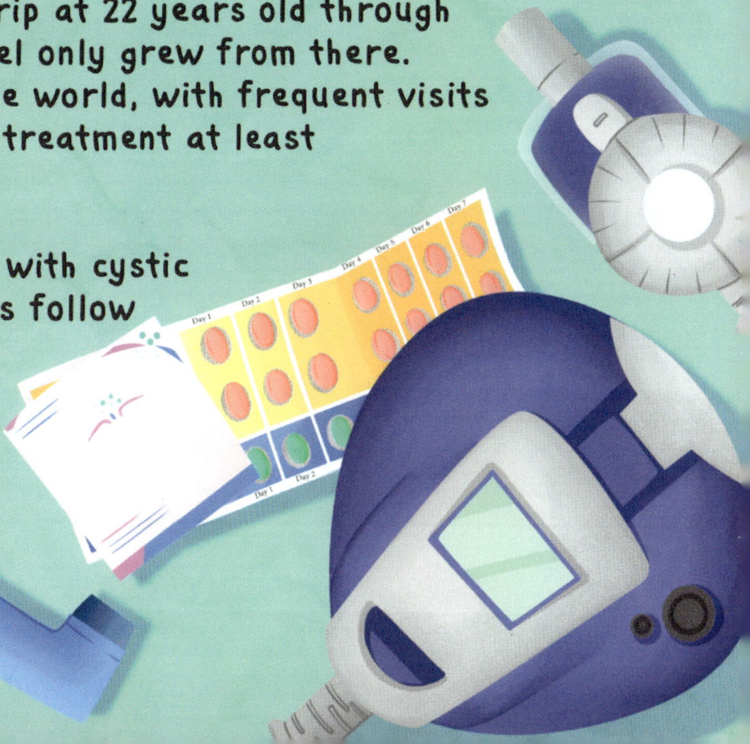

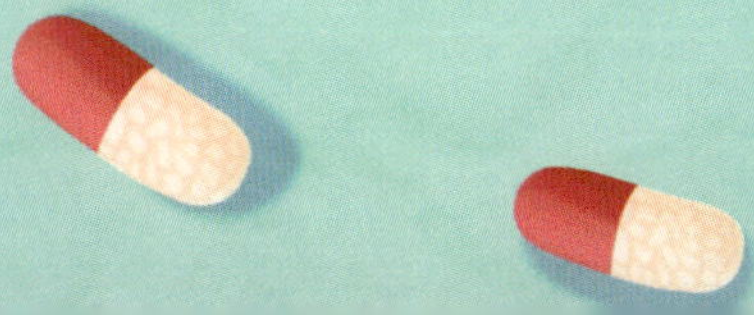

Iceland
North America
USA
France
Africa
South America
n
w
e
s

Europe
Asia
Egypt
Kenya
Australia

Printed in Dunstable, United Kingdom

77088419R00020